A GUIDE

THROUGH

THE WORCESTER

ROYAL PORCELAIN

WORKS.

R. W. BINNS, F.S.A. | E. P. EVANS,
& Secretary.

2/5.

Established 1751.

A GUIDE

Through

The Worcester

Royal Porcelain Works.

Worcester.

1883.

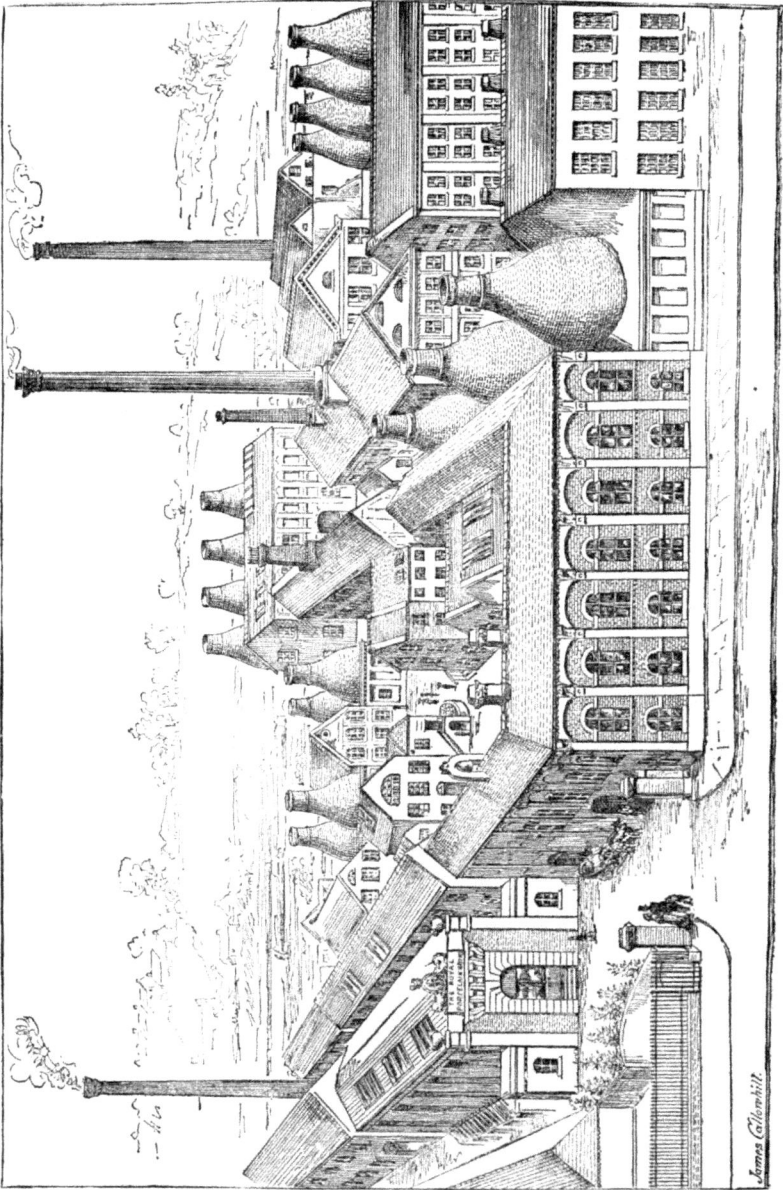

THE WORCESTER ROYAL PORCELAIN WORKS.

James Callowhill.

A GUIDE

THROUGH

THE WORCESTER

ROYAL PORCELAIN

WORKS.

R. W. BINNS, F.S.A.,
Managing Director.

E. P. EVANS,
Manager & Secretary.

James Callowhill. 1882.

THE PRODUCTIONS OF

The Worcester

Royal Porcelain Works

MAY BE OBTAINED

OF THE

Principal China Dealers

THROUGHOUT THE WORLD.

The Public is particularly requested to observe that the productions of the ROYAL PORCELAIN WORKS bear this REGISTERED TRADE MARK, either impressed in the Ware or printed upon the Glaze.

The words—"THE ROYAL PORCELAIN WORKS,"—"THE ROYAL PORCELAIN WORKS, WORCESTER," and "THE WORCESTER ROYAL PORCELAIN WORKS," are also registered as Trade Marks, and are sometimes used upon ware for Government Contracts, &c.

In consequence of the increasing number of Visitors desirous of seeing the process of China Manufacture, it has become necessary to re-arrange the conditions under which they can do so.

Since April 1st, 1880, a charge of Sixpence has been made for each Visitor, who is entitled to a " Guide Book."

This arrangement is made solely with a view to secure better attention for Visitors, and to remove any pretence for the acceptance of Gratuities by the Employés of the Company, who are strictly forbidden to receive any fee or reward.

The Museum, containing specimens of Old Worcester China, may be seen upon application and presentation of address card at the Show Room.

Any complaint of inattention or incivility addressed to the Manager will be promptly dealt with.

VIEW OF THE MUSEUM.

James Carlonhill 1882.

DESCRIPTION OF ILLUSTRATIONS.

The View of the Works is based on a photograph taken from the tower of the Cathedral. The site is that of the establishment founded by Messrs. Chamberlain, some portion of which at one time belonged to Dr. Wall when a partner in Warmstry House. Of the buildings erected by Messrs. Chamberlain some still remain, but the greater part have been replaced by larger workshops and warehouses, to meet extended business and modern requirements. The first important addition was made in 1840, when the union took place between Flight and Barr and Chamberlain; the next in 1851-52-53, under Kerr and Binns; and more recently and much more extensively under the present Company since 1862.

The Museum contains specimens of Worcester Porcelain of all periods arranged chronologically, from the commencement in 1751 to the present time. Also a collection of Japanese Pottery and Porcelain, Enamels and Bronzes, to illustrate some peculiarities of Japanese manufactures.

The Mill.—The first floor is shown, where the large pans for grinding stone and flint, and also the glaze and colour pans, are placed.

Slip House.—The Slip House arrangements may appear to the visitor rather complicated, from the number of pumps, sifters, and presses which are employed; but the description we have given of the process will, we trust, be sufficient to make it understood.

The Thrower.—We have given two illustrations of this branch of the art. The Egyptian thrower is copied from the Theban mural painting as given by Birch, Brongniart, and other authorities. The English thrower shows the present English system.

The Pressing Shop gives a general view of one of the workshops in the Royal Porcelain Works. All kinds of pressed and ordinary useful wares are made here—soup tureens and covered dishes, &c., for dinner services, comports for dessert services, teapots, jugs, and the various etceteras for the breakfast table, all belong to this department.

Ornamental Pottery.—This definition includes figure making, vase making, and the countless variety of decorative works which come under this head, including flower making and piercing.

The Oven is always a subject of interest to the scientific observer, particularly when the great heat required in a porcelain furnace is explained. To judge and control this power requires much experience, nerve, and skill.

The Interior of the Oven is very instructive, as it shews the positions suitable for the various wares. Some will bear more fire than others, and are consequently put in hotter places. Plates will bear more fire than cups, cast ware than pressed ware. It is the business of the fireman to see that each seggar is put in its proper place.

The Dipping Room.—The action of the dipper shows the ordinary process in glazing useful wares. All ornamental goods are subject to the same treatment, requiring somewhat more careful trimming afterwards. The ware having been dipped is placed in a stove to dry. It is then taken by the trimmer, who removes any superfluous glaze, after which it is fired.

The Painting and Gilding Room.—This room is selected as being easy of access, and the workmen being typical of a large number in other parts of the manufactory.

The Printing Room shows the printers at their presses; the transferrers, who place the prints on the wares; and the cutters, who prepare the paper for them.

The Burnishing Room, where the ware is received from the Enamel Kilns, shows the women at work in this department.

Worcester Royal Porcelain Works.

INTRODUCTION.

THE extraordinary mania for Pottery at the present time is not peculiar to our age. The history of our art throughout the world teaches us that it has been cultivated in all ages and under every variety of circumstance, and at times under the most distinguished patronage.

There are many reasons why this important and truly beautiful art should engage the attention of the people. The learned Brongniart says ("Traité des Arts Céramiques")—"I know of no art which presents in the study of its practice, its theory, and its history, so many interesting and varied considerations as the Ceramic art."

We regard it as the graphic medium of antiquity. The clay so sensitive in the hands of the potter exhibits the most subtle expression of the actor's will, and presents to us the mind and character of ancient peoples who may have left no other trace behind.

Birch says—"The history of the art of working in clay, from its rise amongst the oldest nations of antiquity till the present time, resolves itself into two great divisions, which have engaged the attention of two distinct classes of enquirers, namely, the technical or scientific part, comprising all the details of material, manipulation and processes; and, secondly, the historical portion, which embraces not only the history of the art itself, and the application of ancient literature to its elucidation, but also on account of the light thrown by monuments in clay on the history of mankind."[*]

The study, therefore, is neither deficient in dignity, nor limited to trifling investigations, nor rewarded with insignificant results.

A knowledge of the origin and progress of any branch of art must always be of immense importance to its future development and improvement. This is particularly true of the art of working in clay, both from its universal diffusion and from the indestructible nature of its products.

Entirely sympathising with these sentiments, the present *brochure* has been written, not with the idea of giving a history of porcelain manufacture in its technical or scientific details, nor the history of the art with reference to nations, but for the purpose of answering the questions so frequently put by visitors, respecting the various processes of manufacture at the Worcester Royal Porcelain Works.

Everyone being interested in the manufacture of porcelain, it is our desire to explain the processes in the most simple manner, and to endeavour to make a visit instructive as well as interesting, and possibly direct attention to the geological, chemical, and technical studies which are involved in its practice.

The manufactures of the Worcester Royal Porcelain Works embrace the following varieties :—

> Fine Porcelain.
> Ivory Porcelain, a speciality.
> Vitreous Stone Ware (semi-porcelain), a speciality.
> Crown Ware, a speciality.
> Parian.
> Majolica.
> Terra Cotta.
>   &c., &c., &c.

* Birch. " Ancient Pottery and Porcelain."

The raw materials consist of—

China Clay, from Cornwall.
China Stone ,, Cornwall.
Felspar ,, Sweden.
Fireclay ,, Stourbridge.
Do. ,, Broseley.
Marl ,, Broseley.
Flint ,, Dieppe and Gravesend.
Calcined Bones, both home and American.
&c., &c., &c.

The styles of decoration in use at the Royal Porcelain Works embrace all those usual on pottery and porcelain. The following are specialities more or less peculiar to these Works :—

Perforated Porcelain.
Ivory Porcelain.
Raphaelesque Decoration.
Bronze and Metallic Decoration, in various styles.
Jewelled Porcelain.
Enamels on Royal Blue (Worcester enamels).
Modelled and Coloured Golds, as Exhibited at Paris in 1878.

Visitors to the Royal Porcelain Works desirous of seeing the processes of manufacture are conducted over the Works in the following order :—

The Mill.	Biscuit Oven.
The Throwing and Turn-ing Room.	Dipping Room.
	Glost Oven.
Figure Making Room.	Painting and Gilding Rooms.
Burnishing Room.	

THE MILL.

THIS department consists of a boiler-house, engine-house, and the mill, a three-storied building. On the ground floor are placed the washing-pans, which receive the materials from the upper stories, and the arks where the ground substances are stored.

On the first floor are large pans for grinding flint, felspar, Cornish stone, &c., &c., also pans for grinding the glazes, and a series of smaller ones for colours. Adjoining these is the Mixing Room.

On the upper storey are similar large pans for grinding calcined bones, a substance extensively used in the manufacture of china, mills for grinding gold, and a series of pans for grinding colours. The room adjoining is the Laboratory.

The pans are all formed on the same model, but vary in size according to the material for which they are required. They average about 10 feet in diameter and 3 feet in depth. These vats or pans, which are very firmly hooped together, are paved with small blocks of hard chert stone, cemented together with ground china or similar material; in the centre moves an upright shaft, to which are fixed four very strong arms radiating in curved lines, and which move the runners or grinding stones. When the materials to be ground are thrown into the pan, water is supplied to the depth of several inches, and on the mill being put in motion the particles are abraded against each other and between the runners and pavers until they are reduced to the consistence of thick cream.

THE MILL.

As the future beauty of the porcelain depends to a great extent on the proper grinding of the materials, much attention is paid to this department.

The time necessary for grinding the different materials varies from twelve hours to six days; an idea of the fineness required in the grinding may be understood from the inspection of the silk lawn, which numbers about 4,000 meshes to the square inch, and through which every particle of the material used in the body or glaze must pass in the process of mixing.

The principal substances used in the manufacture of porcelain are china clay, china stone, calcined flints, felspar, and calcined bones. For the glazes—borax, lead, flint, Cornish stone, &c., &c.

CHINA CLAY.—Kaolin was first discovered in England by Cookworthy in 1768. It is the felspar of decomposed granite rock, and is found in Cornwall. According to analysis its average composition is—

Silica,	46.
Alumnia,	40.
Lime and Potash,	4.
Water,	10.

It is washed from the decomposed rock and allowed to settle in large vats, from which it is cut in blocks when dry and packed on board ship or in hogsheads for transport to the potteries.

CORNISH STONE.—Petuntse is the decomposed granite rock found in Cornwall. It is composed of quartz, felspar partially decomposed, and a talcose material. It is quarried at St. Stephen's, in Cornwall, and is sent to the various potteries without any preparation.

FLINTS, although they may not be used in the body of the porcelain, are necessary in the manufacture. For pottery purposes boulder flints are preferred, as they are generally more free from lime than chalk flints. In order to prepare them they are placed in a kiln constructed for the purpose and calcined at a red heat; when cool they become perfectly white; in this state they are crushed and ground like the other materials.

CALCINED BONES are largely used in the manufacture of English porcelain. For this purpose ox bones only are suitable. They are brought in large quantities from South America. Home-prepared bones are also used in certain proportions. These latter still retain a proportion of carbon which gives a dark colour to the porcelain clay, but this all disappears in the burning of the ware.

The use of bones is peculiar to English porcelain, and constitutes the great difference between it and the porcelain made on the Continents of Europe and Asia. From the fact of this material being used, the English ware may be called a soft or tender porcelain, and that of France, Germany, and China, hard porcelain.*

For most purposes the artificial or tender porcelain is the better article, particularly for the finer branches of ornamental work and for richly decorated services.

FELSPAR, one of the materials which is much employed, is brought from Sweden in its purest state. It is found in many parts of England and Ireland, but is too often stained with iron. This spar in its raw state is of a salmon-red tint, but becomes pure white on being calcined. It is then ground as we have described.

The materials for the GLAZE of English porcelain are ground flint, Cornish stone, borax, lead, &c. These having been weighed out in proper proportions, are put in a melting furnace, called a fritt kiln. When perfectly melted together they form a glass, which, in a melting state, is allowed to run into a reservoir of water, which disintegrates the mass, and allows the grinding to be more easily performed. A certain proportion of this fritt powder is used along with borax and other materials, which are all ground together, requiring sometimes ten days for the process.

Adjoining the Mill are the Clay Shed and Mixing House or Slip House.

---

* Brongniart divides soft porcelain into two classes—naturally soft and artificially soft. The early pastes of Bow and Chelsea, St. Cloud, and Sèvres were naturally soft ; those of England at the present time are artificially soft.

The CLAY SHED contains stocks of the various clays which do not require grinding, but which are sufficiently pulverised in the state in which they are received. In this shed are several vats containing blungers, which are worked by machinery. These vats are supplied with the different materials, and when sufficiently blunged so as to form a uniform mass like thick cream, the slip (as it is called) is allowed to run into the arks or reservoirs prepared for its reception in the next room, which is called the Mixing Room or

SLIP HOUSE.

Underneath the floor of this building are large arks, which act as reservoirs for the substances from the mill and clay house. Here are the mixing pots, into which the ground materials are thrown by pumps. In the mixing pot is a shaft from which radiate arms having arranged on them rows of magnets which work through the materials so as to remove any particles of iron that may by accident or abrasion have got into them. From the mixing vat the material passes through a series of sieves worked by machinery. It is then pumped into the clay press. This is a machine where the slip is received into a number of chambers lined with linen bags, and where by hydraulic pressure the water is expressed until the mass assumes the consistency of paste. The clay from the press, being in a state of paste or dough, is taken to a vault or clay cellar, where it is regularly beaten and turned over and again beaten and kneaded to make it tough.

When the proper consistency and homogeneity have thus been imparted to the dough it is ready for the workman. The usual methods of manufacture are three—"throwing," "pressing," and "casting,"—the two former with the clay in a state of paste, the latter when in a state of slip.

THE THROWER—THE POTTER'S WHEEL.

Plain circular articles, such as cups and bowls, and in some cases, jugs and teapots, &c., are made on the potter's wheel by the thrower. This apparatus is of great antiquity. It is certainly the oldest mechanical contrivance in connection with the art of pottery.

In the tombs at Thebes (dating about 3,800 years ago) have been discovered drawings which exhibit the potter's art in a variety of forms—the kneader of the clay, the baller, and the thrower.

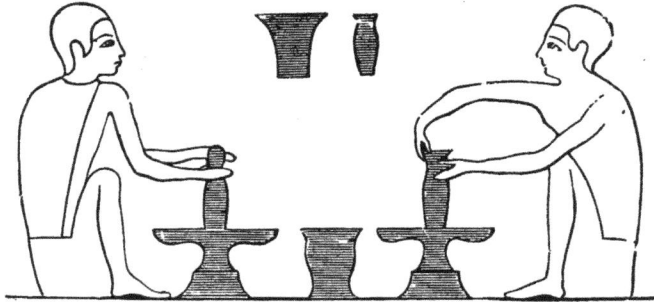

THE EGYPTIAN THROWER.

The man who works at the potter's wheel is called the thrower. He receives from his assistant a ball of clay, which he throws upon the head of the wheel or horizontal lathe before him and presses it with both hands ; the rotary movement causes the clay to rise in the form of a stalk or cone which he then depresses and again allows to rise. When the clay is thus made ready he inserts his thumb into the mass, moulding and fashioning the outsides with the other hand. In this way cups and bowls are formed. In the drawing to which we have alluded the action of the thrower is precisely the same as at the present time. The only difference being in the motive power which turns the wheel. In Egypt it was given by the left hand applied directly to the wheel. In China the motion is given in various ways—by the hand, by the foot, and by a loose strap. On the Continent of Europe, by the foot of the workman.

THE ENGLISH THROWER

illustrates the usual English system. At the Royal Porcelain Works, and at most of the large manufactories, steam power is now used, and the thrower regulates the speed of the wheel by a motion of his foot.

THROWING AND TURNING ROOM.

Formerly all cups and hollow pieces, as jugs and teapots, were made on the wheel; in modern times the greater part of these objects are made in moulds, which not only ensure correctness of size but admit of patterns being embossed on the surface without extra labour to the workman.

THE THROWER having formed the cup or "lining,"* as it is called, afterwards presses it into a mould. In a short time this mould will have absorbed sufficient moisture from the clay to allow it to become detached; it is then taken out and is ready for

THE TURNER.

THE TURNER fixes the ware upon his lathe and treats it much the same as he would a piece of wood or metal. He finishes the edge and foot, and if necessary the outside surface. Having completed the form of the cup it is passed to the Handler.

Handles are pressed in moulds, and whether for tea-cups or vases, undergo the same process of trimming and fitting, which is speedily done by the workman, who next proceeds to fix it on the cup with a little liquid clay called slip. This clay acts as a cement, and being of the same material, unites the two parts when burnt in the oven. All objects with handles go through a similar process.

The manufacture of plates and dishes is called FLAT PRESSING, and the process is very different from that just described.

For plates the clay is weighed into balls, which are beaten out into flat circles like pancakes. The mould that gives the form to the face of the plate or saucer is fixed on a horizontal lathe called a jigger. It is then covered with a disc of clay and pressed firmly on to the mould whilst it revolves very quickly. The workman then takes a tool called a profile fitted to the edge of the

*The Articles formed by the Thrower in the presence of visitors are made to show the power and working of the Potter's Wheel, but are of no use as manufactured articles, cups being made in moulds, and saucers by a process afterwards described as flat pressing.

PRESSING ROOM.

mould, and which on being pressed in the centre causes the foot to rise in a perfect circle. The mould, with the plate upon it, is next placed in the stove to dry. When the heat causes the plate to contract from the mould it is taken off and finished in a semi-dry state. The plate is then ready to be burned, and the mould is ready to receive another charge.

The manufacture of soup tureens, covered dishes, ewers and basins, &c., is called HOLLOW WARE PRESSING. These objects are all made in moulds. The workman first prepares a slab of clay, and having carefully placed it in the mould he bosses it with a wet sponge, and presses it into every line of the pattern. The mould after a little time absorbs sufficient moisture to allow the clay to contract, and the piece is easily removed.

ORNAMENTAL PRESSING ROOM.

ORNAMENTAL POTTERY.

CASTING, one of the most interesting processes of potting, is shown in the *Figure Making Department*.

When a figure of any size or shape has been finished by the modeller it is cut into pieees to be moulded. The mould maker is most careful to arrange that each part shall be delivered from the mould in perfect condition and with as little seam as possible. A figure when thus cut up and moulded may be represented by from twenty to thirty moulds, each containing a separate part.

The china for this process of manufacture is not used in a clay state, but as a liquid slip like thick cream. This is poured into the orifice of the mould left for the purpose, and then allowed to stand for a short time ; when sufficient slip has adhered to the mould the remainder is poured back into the casting jug. The slip having remained in the mould for some minutes becomes sufficiently solid to enable the workman to handle it. He next proceeds to arrange all the pieces on a slab of plaster before him. He then trims the superfluous clay from each, and applies some liquid slip to the parts and so makes a perfect joint, each part being fitted to its proper place, until the whole figure is built up as it was before it was moulded ; as each joint is made the superfluous slip is removed with a camel's hair pencil.

The object is next propped with various strips of clay having exactly the same shrinkage, and is then ready for the oven.

This shrinkage or contraction to which we have alluded is one of the most important changes, as well as one of the greatest difficulties encountered in the art of pottery.

The change will be more or less, according to the materials used and the process employed in making. Thus, earthenware will not contract so much as porcelain, and a pressed piece will not contract so much as a cast one.* The contractions are sufficiently well known to the modeller, and he makes allowance

* The shrinkage arises from two causes ; first, from the loss of water which in a highly plastic paste may cause contraction to the extent of upwards of 15 per cent. : and, secondly, if the body be formed of readily fusible substances a further diminution of bulk arises from the closer juxtaposition of the component particles by incipient fusion, and this amounts frequently to from 10 to 15 per cent.

in the model accordingly, the design being fashioned so much
larger than is actually required ; the shrinkage from the original
model to the finished object being sometimes equal to 25 per cent.

The ware up to this point in all the stages of manufacture we
have described is most tender, and can only be handled with the
greatest care.

BISCUIT KILN AND PLACING HOUSE.

The manufactured objects being now ready for baking are
taken to the placing house of the biscuit oven, where may be seen
some hundreds of seggars, of all shapes and sizes.   These
seggars, which are made of fire-clay, and are very strong, are the
cases in which the ware is to be burned.   Common brown wares,
when the fire is comparatively easy, may be burned without any
protection, as the fire or the smoke cannot injure them ; but for
porcelain or white earthenware these cases are necessary.

The seggars are made of various shapes to suit the different
wares.   Flat round ones are used for plates, each china plate

requiring its own seggar and its own bed in it, made of ground flint very carefully prepared, for the china plate will take the exact form made in the bed of flint.

Cups and bowls are placed, a number of them together, in oval seggars, ranged on china rings to keep them straight. These rings must be properly covered with flint to prevent them adhering to the ware burned upon them.

The seggars when full are piled one over the other most carefully in the oven, so as to allow the pressure to be equalized as much as possible; this is absolutely necessary, as when the oven is heated to a white heat the least irregularity of bearing might cause a pile to topple on one side and possibly affect the firing of the whole oven causing a great amount of loss.

INTERIOR OF BISCUIT OVEN.

Calcined flint is used for the purpose of making beds for the ware, because being pure silica it has no melting properties, and will not adhere to the china.

The form of china ovens seems to have been much the same in all ages, viz., that of a cone or large bee-hive.

A china oven is generally about 14 feet in diameter inside. It is built of fire bricks, and is encased several times round with bands of iron to prevent too great expansion from the heat inside. There are generally eight fireplaces around the oven with flues which lead directly into the oven in different directions.

A china oven takes about forty hours to fire ; it is then left to cool for about forty-eight hours.

In order to test the burning, the fireman draws small test-cups through holes in different parts of the oven made for the purpose. These tests show both by contraction and the various degrees of translucency the progress of the fire. The test holes are carefully stopped with bricks so that cold air cannot be drawn into the oven.

The porcelain having been burnt is now in a state called biscuit ; it is translucent and perfectly vitreous. Having had the flint rubbed off the surface and been carefully examined it is sent into

THE DIPPING ROOM.

The dipping room is supplied with large tubs of the various glazes suitable to the different kinds of ware.

The glaze is really a glass, which is so chemically prepared of borax, lead, flint, &c., &c., that when burned it will adhere to the porcelain and will not craze or crackle on the surface.

This glaze is ground very fine (being on the mill for about ten days) until it assumes the consistency of cream.

The process of glazing is simple, but requires a practised hand, so that every piece may be equally glazed and the glaze itself equally distributed over the surface.

THE DIPPING ROOM.

From the dipping room the ware is brought into the drying stove, where the glaze is dried on the ware. It is then taken by women into the trimming room, where any superfluous glaze is taken off and defective places are made good. From this room it is taken to the glost oven placing house, where the greatest care and cleanliness are required, as should any dust or foreign substance get on the glaze it will adhere in the fire and very likely spoil the piece.

The glost oven is of the same construction as the biscuit. It takes 16 hours to fire, and the tests are made in the same manner as in the biscuit oven. In about 36 hours the oven will be sufficiently cool for the ware to be removed. It is then sent into the White Warehouse, where it is sorted and stored until required for decoration by the painters and gilders.

Visitors generally look forward with pleasure to the mysteries of the Decorating Department. It is interesting to watch the painters, some engaged on landscapes, others on birds, or flowers, or butterflies. All are interested in their work, which to the uninitiated may appear. at first sight to be very unpromising, the colours being dull and the drawing unfinished. As the work advances it will be better understood. After the first " wash in " has been burned and the painter has worked upon it for the second fire, the forms and finish both in style and colour begin to appear.

The colours used are all made from metallic oxides ; thus copper gives green and black ; cobalt, blue ; gold, purple ; iron, red ; &c.

The painters are trained from about 14 years of age under special instructors, they thus acquire a facility of drawing and general manipulation of the colours which it is found almost impossible to attain at a later period of life.

The gilding process is carried on in rooms adjacent to the painting. The elaborate and finely executed patterns in gold are all traced by the hand. The workmen require special training for this department also, correct drawing and clean finish being absolutely necessary. For the purpose of getting correct circles and speedy finish on circular pieces a simple mechanical contrivance is used. A small table or stand with a revolving head receives the plate, or saucer, or cup, which is carefully centered so as to run truly. The workman then having filled his pencil with gold, fixes his hand upon his rest, applies the pencil to the edge of the piece, and gently turns the table head round ; the edge is thus formed in a moment in the most perfect manner.

The gold used for decorating porcelain is the purest that can be obtained from the assayer. It is supplied to the factory in brown grains like ground coffee.

The chemist then mixes with it a little flux to make it adhere to the ware, and a proportion of quicksilver (which all flies off in the kiln) to reduce it for grinding. It is next ground on a mill for about thirty hours, and it is ready for the workman.

DECORATING ROOM.

As seen in use it looks more like printer's ink than precious gold; its true character is revealed after it has passed through the enamel kiln.

As nearly every process of decorating porcelain is performed on the glazed surface of the ware, special kilns are arranged for burning the colours and gold that they may adhere or sink into the glaze. In proportion as this operation is properly performed so will the colours be more or less bright and beautiful. The kilns used for this purpose may properly be called muffles, as they are similar in principle to those used by goldsmiths, only much larger in size. They are heated on the reverberating principle, the fire-places (which vary in number according to the size of the kiln) being at the side, and the flues going round the kiln.

Great care is required in placing the ware in its finished state. as any particle of dirt, or the mark of a dirty finger, or a rub on colour or gold will all be shown on drawing the ware, and will necessitate another firing and consequent additional risk.

The Worcester Porcelain Works were the first to introduce printing on porcelain with any amount of success. The process has been continued ever since the year 1756, but the character of the work has been to some extent altered. In the early days of its introduction it was principally used to print patterns in cobalt blue in imitation of Chinese painted patterns. It was also much used, and probably in its earliest days, as a means of decorating objects with fine line engravings in black or red, and in such cases the object came finished from the printer's press. Printing is still used in this manner for common wares, but in the Worcester Works it is generally employed to give the outline to a pattern, and by this means save the trouble in drawing, the colouring of the pattern being done by other hands, principally females.

Printed patterns pass through the enamel kiln fire like other decorative processes.

The time required for enamel kiln firing is about six hours.

THE PRINTING ROOM.

James Callowhill.

BURNISHING AND CHASING.

When the ware is drawn from the enamel kiln it is carefully sorted. That which has to be re-painted or re-gilt is sent to its proper destination, and that which is finished is sent into the Burnishing Room, where it is distributed to a number of women who perform this last operation. The gold is now of a dull yellow colour, but after it has been carefully cleaned and a burnisher of bloodstone or agate has been quickly rubbed over it, it assumes the beautiful bright appearance of burnished gold.

When patterns are chased upon the gold, a tool with a fine point formed of agate is used, by which only those parts to be polished are touched, leaving the dead gold to show a relief in colour.

From the burnishing room the ware is sent into the warehouse, where it is distributed to the various orders for which it has been made. It is then papered up and packed.

The visitors having now been conducted through the various representative* departments of the manufactory, and having seen how the meanest material in nature, "clay," can be made to assume the most beautiful forms, and by the application and combination of science and art to become more valuable than the precious metal itself, will, we feel assured, be more ready to appreciate the finished article, whether in the form of a simple cup and saucer or plate, or the most elaborately-decorated vase.

Shaw, when writing on Staffordshire pottery, says—" To give our readers some idea of the various ramifications of a single piece of *earthenware* before it arrives at completion, we may note that at the present day to produce the commonest painted bowl used by the poorest peasant wife to contain the breakfast for her rustic

---

* The workshops exhibited are selected as being the most likely to interest, whilst they are types of many others. The rooms in which the higher classes of decoration are carried on are not shown, as the interruption of visitors would disturb the artists at their work.

THE BURNISHING ROOM.

James Callowhill 1884

husband, the clays of Dorset and Devonshire, the flints of Kent, the granite of Cornwall, the lead of Montgomery, the manganese of Warwickshire, and the soda of Cheshire must be conveyed from their respective districts, and by the ingenious processes, the results of unnumbered experiments, be made to combine with other substances apparently as heterogeneous, obtained from other nations."

"An ordinary piece of ware will pass through, on the average, at least 18 different hands or processes, after the materials arrive on the ground, before it can be sent out in a perfect state, viz., the miller, the slip maker, the preparer of clay, the baller, the thrower, the carrier, the turner, the handler, the biscuit fireman, the scourer, the dipper, the glost fireman, the sorter, the printer, the painter, the gilder, the enamel fireman, the burnisher."

The Worcester enamels on Royal blue, painted *en gresaille*, have been considered amongst the finest porcelain works produced in England. The idea for this work was taken from the enamels of Limoges executed on copper in the 16th century. The pictures by Penicaud (who painted about the year 1503) are those which have been studied for style. There is more delicacy in his light and shade and more careful drawing of the figure than in the productions of the other enamellers of his time.

These works in enamel are quite different in their treatment to ordinary porcelain painting, the enamel being thick and opaque, and the principal lights and shades being given by the different thicknesses of the enamel.

In figure subjects, landscapes, flowers, and decorations, we must consider the paintings on the *pâte tendre* of old Sèvres as the *beau ideal* of porcelain painting.

The Sèvres vase was coated with a glaze so rich and soft that when painted and subjected to the enamel kiln fire the colours literally sank into the glaze without deterioration. It then appeared as if the vase had been painted on the biscuit and the glaze passed over it, a process which at that time would have been an impossibility, because the fire necessary to melt the glaze would have destroyed the tender colours. The paintings on the old Sèvres vases have been executed with such high artistic feeling, and the vases themselves are so truly illustrative of that most decorative of styles, the Louis XV., that we do not at all wonder they are highly appreciated and command almost fabulous prices. Vases after this manner are painted at Worcester with various coloured grounds—Royal blue, rose du Barry, turquoise, &c.

In addition to these painted and coloured vases there are other styles of decorated porcelain. A style called Raphaelesque was introduced at the exhibition of 1862. It consisted principally in colouring embossed surfaces after the manner of the "Capo di Monte," but with this difference, the "Capo di Monte" was a cold white porcelain, that of Worcester was of a soft ivory tone which tended to harmonize the colours and enrich their effect.

The ivory porcelain we have alluded to in the above description, has been a speciality of Worcester since 1856, and has been the means of introducing several varieties of decorated wares. United with the Celadon it makes a very elegant combination either for figures or vases.

To the admirers of colour, the Persian turquoise, Imperial yellow, mauve, celeste, and other enamels present an interesting series, which until recently have not been produced on pottery.

A recent novelty in taste is the adoption of Japanese style throughout nearly the entire series of manufacture. The manner in which this has been introduced at Worcester is quite original. The first general display of the style was made at the Vienna Exhibition in 1873, where it received the highest award in the Diploma of Honour.

The great novelty in the character of these designs is based upon the *ivory porcelain*, which forms a delicate tinted ground for the bronzes and coloured golds, another feature in the new treatment.

It is unnecessary here to defend a style which has found so many admirers, but we may express our opinion that where it is best understood it is most appreciated. Many essays have been written upon it. It is certainly not exhausted, and we trust that improved education in decorative art will gain for it, as it deserves, increased admiration.

In writing of Japanese taste we refer to the ancient and best examples, for unfortunately since the style has become fashionable, the country has been inundated with thousands of specimens from Japan, all imitations of the true work, but inferior in material, in execution, and in taste.

In a large manufactory like the Worcester Royal Porcelain Works, there are great varieties of ware always in process of manufacture, and visitors will probably notice the ornamental as more attractive, nevertheless, the variety of styles and patterns in the Service department will be found worthy of attention.

Dinner and Dessert Services, Breakfast and Tea Services, in porcelain form a very large proportion of the manufactures of the establishment.

The porcelain of Worcester has long been celebrated, but to meet the demand for a less expensive article, CROWN WARE (a vitreous body) was introduced a few years ago. This ware has been selected by the Admiralty for the use of the fleet, and is much in demand for regimental messes and clubs.

The difference between CROWN WARE and EARTHENWARE is shown in the fracture, which in the Worcester ware is *vitreous*, it does not absorb grease or moisture, it will not craze, and being very durable is well suited for these special purposes, as well as for general use.

Worcester Porcelain.

THE WORCESTER PORCELAIN WORKS were established in the year 1751. The staple manufactures of the city had been for some years declining; the cloth business had been driven away by unsatisfactory trading; carpets and gloves were still made, but did not afford sufficient occupation for the people; and it was also considered advisable to raise up, by extended manufactures, a body of workmen who should be freemen electors, trained to withstand the Jacobite tendency of the time.

The manufacture of Porcelain was engaging the attention of the Princes of Europe, it was enjoying a reputation in England at Bow and Chelsea, and its artistic and scientific labours were such as to enlist the sympathies of everyone desirous of improving the trade of the country and the tastes of the people.

Worcester had neither coals, nor clay, nor skilled hands, but "the faithful city" had Dr. Wall, a talented physician, a clever chemist, and an accomplished artist. By his scientific skill he produced one of the most beautiful porcelains in Europe—which is even now the admiration of connoisseurs—and to his judgment and enterprise the concern was indebted for the first 30 years of its success.

The Worcester Company made a fine porcelain from the commencement, and decorated it after the Chinese taste according to the prevailing models. The earliest designs were nearly all painted in blue.

In 1756 transfer printing was introduced, both with finely-engraved black prints on the glaze and with blue prints under the glaze, which could with difficulty be distinguished from the painted subjects.

The styles adopted at Worcester were very varied, but were generally selected from the finest examples of Japanese and Chinese and Dresden manufacture, as well as the very beautiful wares of Sèvres and Chelsea ; but whatever style was produced it was made to bear a Worcester character, and, with the exception of Chelsea, no English works bear evidence of so much loving care in their production. It is certain that from about 1760 to 1775 some extremely beautiful wares were produced both in vases and services. The specimens which have lately been brought to light have never been excelled in England.

Doctor Wall died in 1776, and the remaining partners carried on the works with spirit and success until the year 1783, when the whole establishment was sold to Mr. Flight, of London. The business was conducted by his two sons, Joseph and John, till 1792.

In 1788 George III. visited the Worcester works, and granted his warrant permitting the establishment henceforth to be called "Royal."

In 1793 Mr. Barr joined the concern, and the firm of Flight and Barr commenced. It continued without variation until 1807, when Mr. Barr, jun., was taken into partnership, and the title was altered to Barr, Flight, and Barr, which lasted until 1813. On the death of Mr. Barr, sen., a younger son was taken into partnership, and the firm changed to Flight, Barr, and Barr, which was continued till 1840, although Mr. Flight had died in 1829. The establishment was united to that of Messrs. Chamberlain in the former year (1840).

Mr. Chamberlain, who had been engaged with the original company under Dr. Wall, left the works when they were sold to Mr. Flight, and commenced business on his own account.

The firm from 1786 to 1798 was Robert Chamberlain, sen , Humphrey Chamberlain, and Richard Nash (sleeping partner). From 1798 to 1804 the firm was Humphrey Chamberlain and Robert Chamberlain, jun. From 1804 to 1811, Humphrey Chamberlain, Robert Chamberlain, and Grey Edward Boulton (sleeping partner). From 1811 to 1827, Humphrey Chamberlain and Robert Chamberlain. From 1827 to 1840, Walter Chamberlain and John Lilly.

The united firms in 1840 were constituted a Joint Stock Company—

Walter Chamberlain,	Martin Barr,
John Lilly,	George Barr,

and Fleming St. John, Managing Directors.

The Company was dissolved in 1848, and the firm was again Walter Chamberlain and John Lilly.

In 1850 another change was made, and the style became Walter Chamberlain, Frederick Lilly, and W. H. Kerr.

From 1852 to 1862, W. H. Kerr and R. W. Binns.

In 1862, commenced the present Joint Stock Company.

In the early part of the present century Worcester had few competitors in the manufacture of first-class porcelain. The patronage of the King and Royal Family, which was liberally accorded, stimulated the production of both fine porcelain and artistic productions. A special body called Regent Porcelain was invented by Mr. Chamberlain for the Prince Regent, and obtained great favour from the Court, but being very costly in its production it was discontinued after a few years, other improved bodies taking its place, having equal durability of wear and beauty of appearance.

Messrs. Chamberlain entered largely into the manufacture of porcelain buttons made of dry clay by pressure, but a dispute about the patent in 1850 and the introduction of a similar article from France put an end to the business.

The manufacture of encaustic tiles was al   ntroduced by Messrs. Chamberlain. These had a great and deserved success. This business was transferred to Messrs. Maw in 1851, and by them shortly after removed to Broseley, where the establishment has been greatly extended, and obtained a very high position from the artistic character of its productions.

The second century of the Royal Porcelain Works commenced with a new proprietorship—Mr. Kerr, who had been a partner in the former firm with Mr. Chamberlain and Mr. Lilly, was now joined by Mr. Binns; the buildings of the manufactory were largely extended and considerable progress was made in giving a higher tone to its productions, which received high praise at the Exhibitions of 1853, 1855, and 1862; in the latter year the business was formed into a Joint Stock Company, since which time further large additions have been made to the works, which now employ more than 600 persons, and increased reputation has attended their productions. The highest award (the Diploma of Honour) was obtained at Vienna, and at Paris—the Gold Medal.

The Partnership Deeds of
The Worcester Porcelain Company in 1751.

The original Deeds relating to the formation of this Company in 1751 have recently been discovered. They are very interesting, both in giving the names of the original proprietors, and the terms upon which the company was formed.

Marks on Worcester Porcelain.

CAUTION.—The Directors of the Worcester Royal Porcelain Works consider it necessary to warn the public against imitations of their wares, both *ancient* and *modern*.

The square mark and also the crescent are being copied to a very serious extent on rich patterns with Royal blue and salmon scale ground. These *Forgeries* of old wares are nearly all on French hard-paste porcelain.

Imitations of modern work are being made both at home and abroad, it is therefore important to see that this registered trade mark appears on all wares sold as Worcester Porcelain. It is either impressed in the ware, or printed on the glaze.

In publishing the marks on Worcester Porcelain, the Directors desire to state, for the benefit of collectors, that many of the best specimens of Old Worcester are not marked, and a large number bearing marks of repute are of little value.

The marks given in the following pages have been found upon old Worcester porcelain, but many of them are only copies of Oriental devices. The painter, in copying the patterns from some Oriental piece, has completed his work by copying the device on the back also, but it is evident that such mark was not intended to deceive, as in many cases the Worcester crescent is placed along with it.

Nos. 1, 2, 3, appear on all kinds of Worcester china from 1752 to about 1800.   The crescent is the true Worcester mark ; it was taken from one of the quarterings in the Warmstry arms.

Nos. 4. and 5.—The crescents, with addition are not common ; they are generally on blue ware.

Nos. 6, 7, 8, 9, 10.—The W mark is found on a great variety of patterns of early date.

Nos. 11, 12, 13, are the square marks so much sought after, and at present so freely forged.

Nos. 14, 15.—Also square marks but not so common.

Nos. 16 to 22 are copies of Chinese and Japanese patterns, and generally appear on wares of that class.

Nos. 23 and 24, and 28 and 29, are imitations of the Dresden mark, but they appear on many styles of ware, sometimes even on black print.

Nos. 25, 26, 27, appear only on black transfer prints between 1756 and 1774.

No. 30 has been found impressed in the ware 1783 to 1791.

No. 31.—In blue under glaze for the same period.

No. 32 appears on the Royal service made for the Duke of Clarence.

No. 33.—This letter is found scratched in the clay after Mr. Barr was taken into partnership ; from 1793 to about 1800.

No. 34.—From 1793 to 1807.

Nos. 35 and 37.—From 1807 to 1813.

Nos. 36 and 38.—From 1813 to 1840.

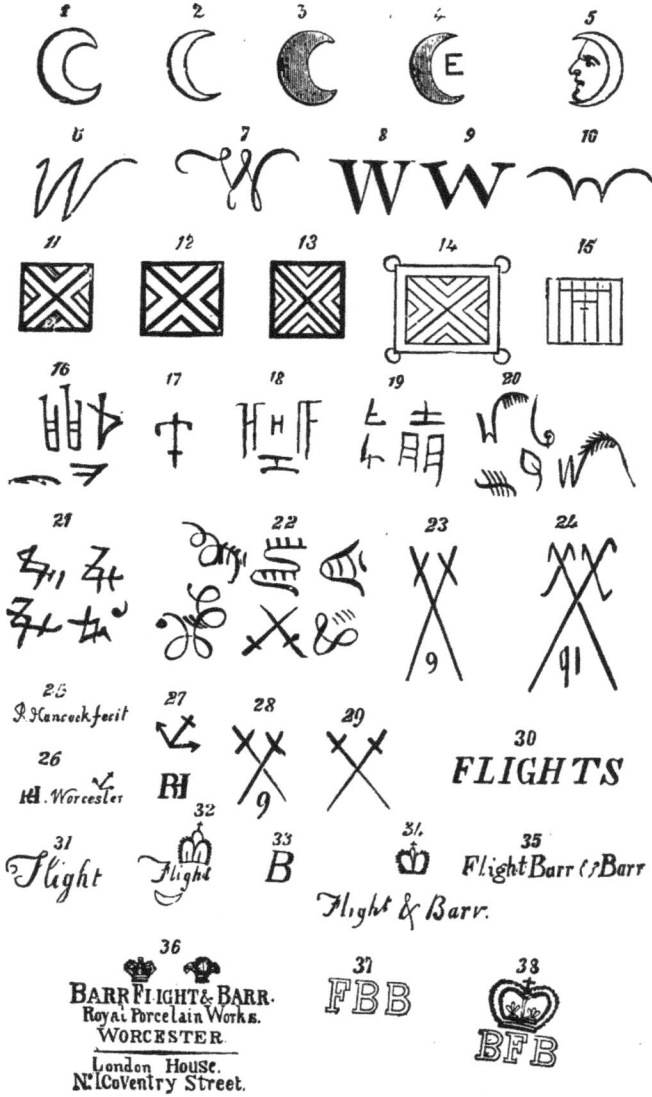

No. 39.—Used by Chamberlains, written with and without "Worcester," from 1788 to about 1804.

No. 40.—Written on specimens in 1814.

No. 41.—Printed mark used from 1814 to about 1820.

No. 42.—Printed mark used from 1820 to 1840.

No. 43.--Printed mark used between 1840 and 1845.

No. 44.—Printed mark used in 1847.

No. 45.—Used between 1847 and 1850 ; sometimes impressed in the ware, and at other times printed upon it.

No. 46.—Mark used in 1850 and 1851.

No. 47.—Mark used by Kerr and Binns from 1852 to 1862.

No. 48.—Mark used by Kerr and Binns on special pieces.

No. 49.—Mark used by the present Company from 1862.

The figures in the concluding series are considered to be workmen's marks, and are generally, if not exclusively, found on blue painted wares.

39

Chamberlain's

40
Chamberlain's
Worcester
& 63, Piccadilly,
London.

41
Chamberlain's,
Regent China,
Worcester
& 155,
New Bond Street
London.

42
Chamberlain's
Worcester;
& 155,
New Bond Street. London
Royal Porcelain Manufacturers.

43
CHAMBERLAIN & CO.,
WORCESTER
155 NEW BOND ST.,
& NO. 1,
COVENTRY ST,
LONDON.

44
Chamberlain & Co.. Worcester.

46
CHAMBERLAIN & Cº
WORCESTER

47
SI

45
CHAMBERLAINS

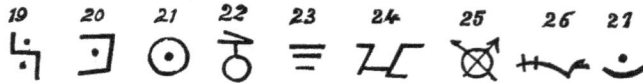

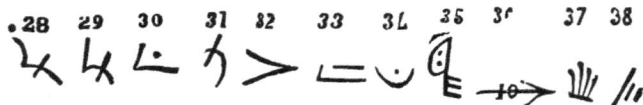

48
K&B

49
W
SI

7   2   3   4   5   6   7   8   9

10   11   12   13   14   15   16   17   18

19   20   21   22   23   24   25   26   27

28   29   30   31   32   33   34   35   36   37   38

Vienna Exhibition, 1873.

THE PRODUCTIONS OF THE

Worcester Porcelain Works,

AT THIS EXHIBITION,

OBTAINED

THE DIPLOMA OF HONOUR

(THE HIGHEST AWARD),

AND

⇀ SEVEN WORKMEN'S MEDALS. ↽

The Exhibits were new in style, a large proportion being founded on Oriental taste.

"For novelty, combined with excellence, I think that the Royal Works of Worcester must this time stand first."—*Standard*, September 30th, 1873.

EXTRACT FROM REPORT

ON

MODERN PORCELAINS

WHICH WERE SHOWN AT THE

Universal Exhibition of 1878,

ADDRESSED TO

THE MINISTER OF INSTRUCTION AND THE FINE ARTS,

BY

M. LAMEIRE,

IN THE NAME OF THE COMMISSION FOR THE

IMPROVEMENT OF THE NATIONAL MANUFACTURE OF SÈVRES.

———————

AVING finished the short review of the French section of the Ceramics, let us enter into the North West side of the Exhibition in the midst of the foreign productions, and commence the comparative review with England.

We must place here highest in rank the productions of the Worcester Manufactory. They are distinguished from all others by skill and accurate judgment in Ceramic Art and by great perfection in the execution. –

The bisque Parian, which reminds us rather of ivory than of marble, draws attention by its whitish yellow tones, upon which foliage and fantastic animals in coloured golds (yellow and green) combine happily with the ground which they decorate.

We must also notice services of simple outlines cleverly pierced.

Let us equally notice large gourd-shaped vases with birds in gold, and foliage of a happy arrangement.

Circular plaques also ornamented in the same manner, but upon grounds of red, black, or green, like Chinese lacquer, obtained by the great fire, show very remarkable results of powerful harmony, which we cannot however approve, when considered as imitations of another material in porcelain. Nor can we approve the long horns of Japanese form encirled by leaves and fruits completely detached, so closely imitating nature as to exclude all sentiment of decorative art.

Having said this, we cannot speak too highly of the charm contained in each of these thousand objects, vases, table, dessert, and tea services, where the ornament is always in harmony with the object decorated.

The foregoing Report having been made for the French Government, and particularly for the advantage of the National Establishment at Sèvres, the Directors of the Worcester Royal Porcelain Works submit it as an unbiassed opinion of their exhibits.

FINIS

BAYLIS, LEWIS AND CO., PRINTERS, NEW STREET, WORCESTER.

www.ingramcontent.com/pod-product-compliance
Lightning Source LLC
Chambersburg PA
CBHW081725270326
41933CB00017B/3300